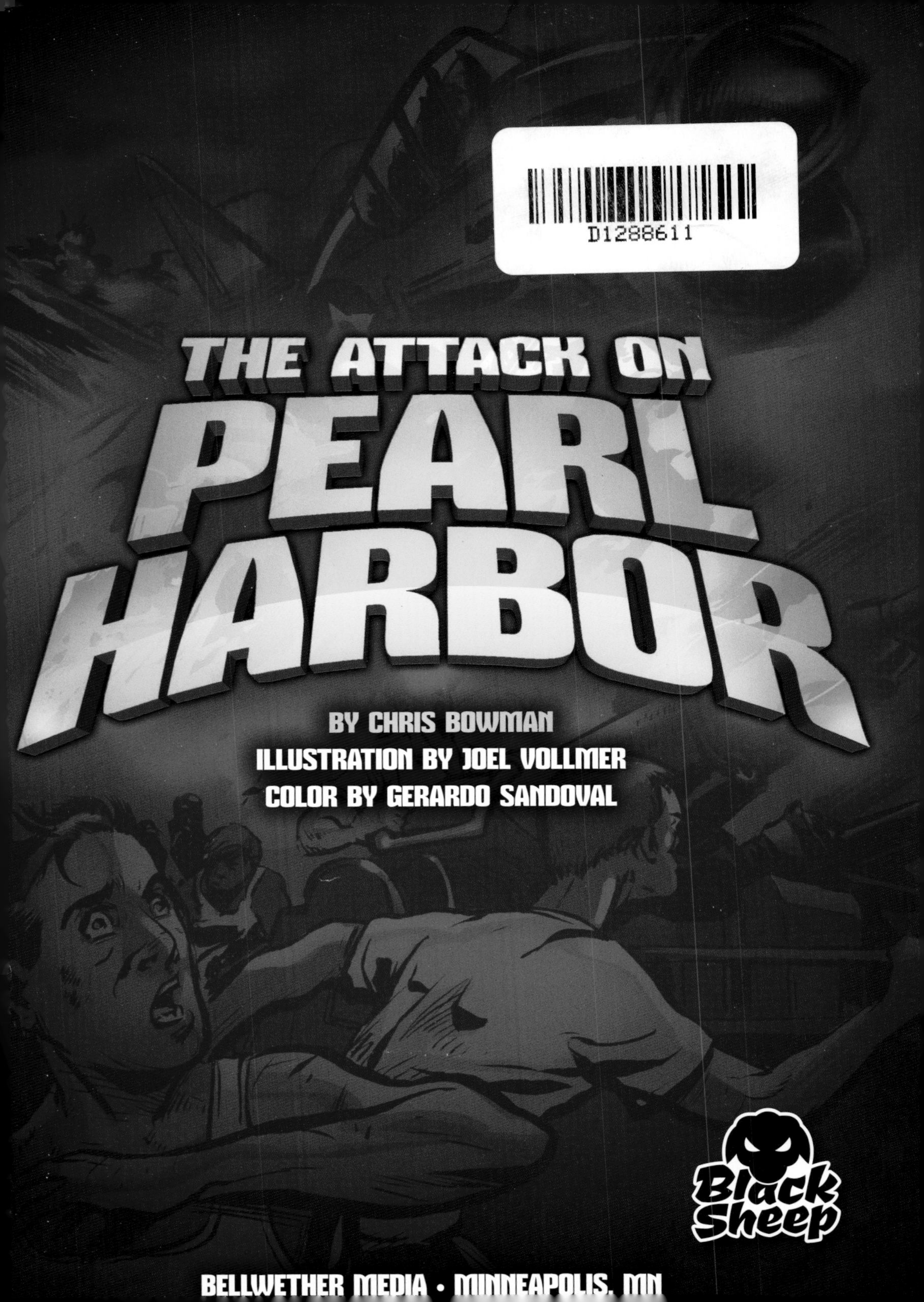

THE ATTACK ON PEARL HARBOR

BY CHRIS BOWMAN
ILLUSTRATION BY JOEL VOLLMER
COLOR BY GERARDO SANDOVAL

Black Sheep
BELLWETHER MEDIA • MINNEAPOLIS, MN

STRAY FROM REGULAR READS
WITH BLACK SHEEP BOOKS.
FEEL A RUSH WITH EVERY READ!

Library of Congress Cataloging-in-Publication Data

Bowman, Chris, 1990-
    The Attack on Pearl Harbor / by Chris Bowman.
        pages cm. -- (Black Sheep: Disaster Stories)
    Includes bibliographical references and index.
    Summary: "Exciting illustrations follow the events of the attack on Pearl Harbor. The combination of brightly colored panels and leveled text is intended for students in grades 3 through 7"-- Provided by publisher.
    ISBN 978-1-62617-150-3 (hardcover : alkaline paper)
    1. Pearl Harbor (Hawaii), Attack on, 1941--Juvenile literature. I. Title.
    D767.92.B67 2014
    940.54'26693--dc23
                                2014009036

This edition first published in 2015 by Bellwether Media, Inc.

Printed in the United States of America, North Mankato, MN.

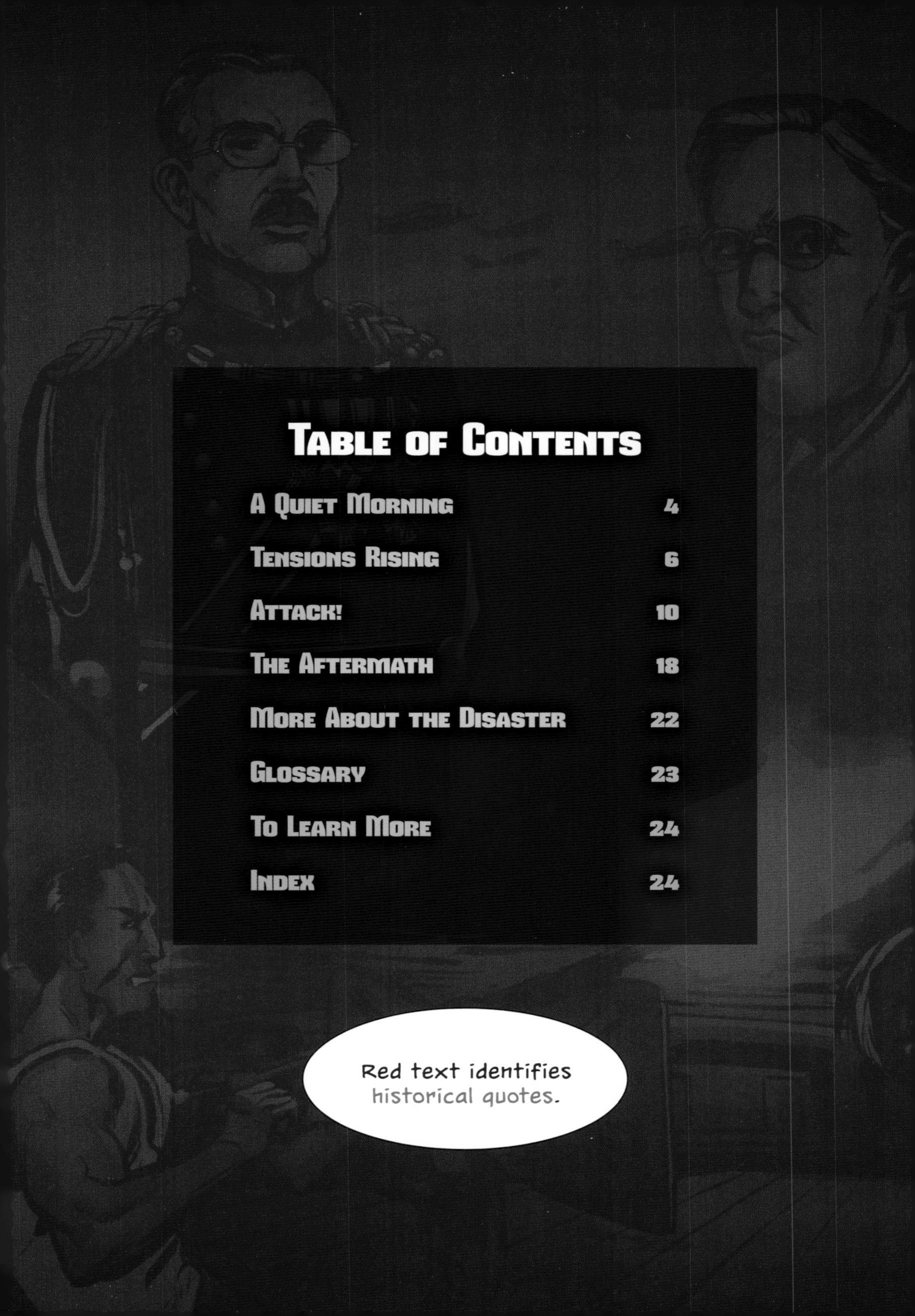

Table of Contents

Red text identifies historical quotes.

A Quiet Morning

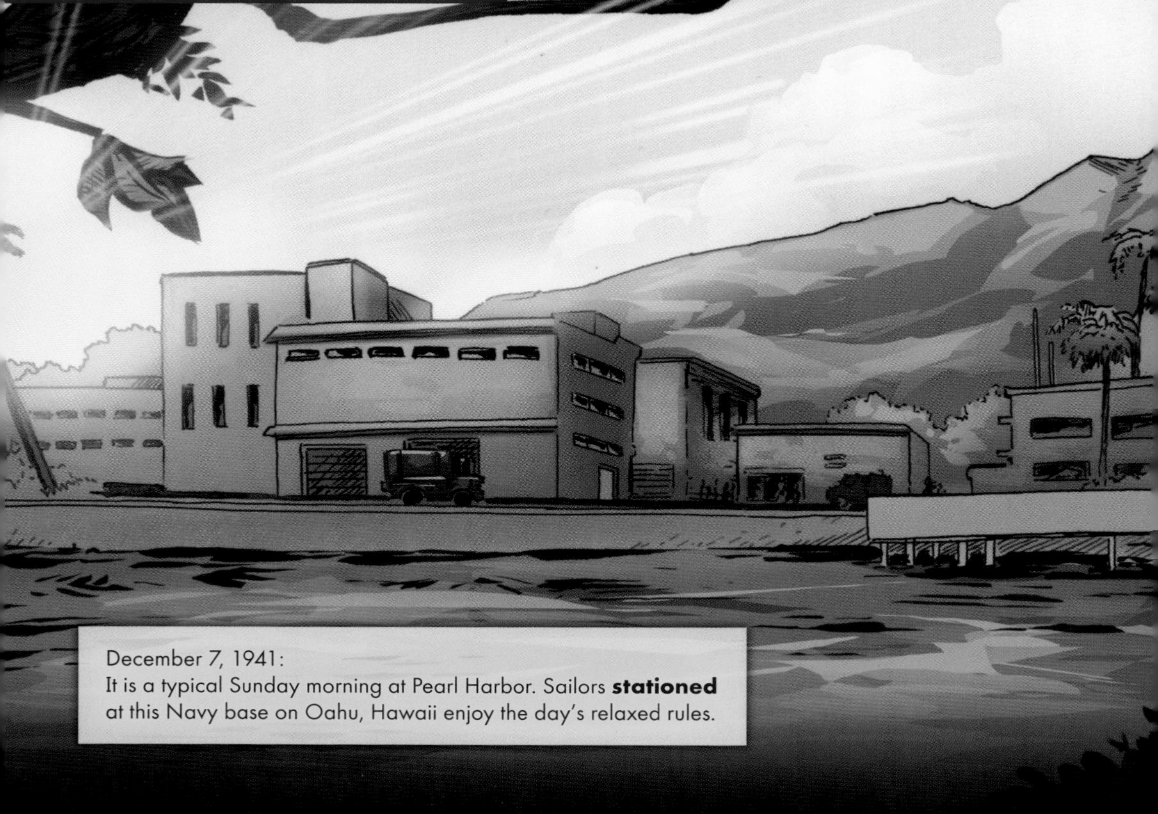
December 7, 1941:
It is a typical Sunday morning at Pearl Harbor. Sailors **stationed** at this Navy base on Oahu, Hawaii enjoy the day's relaxed rules.

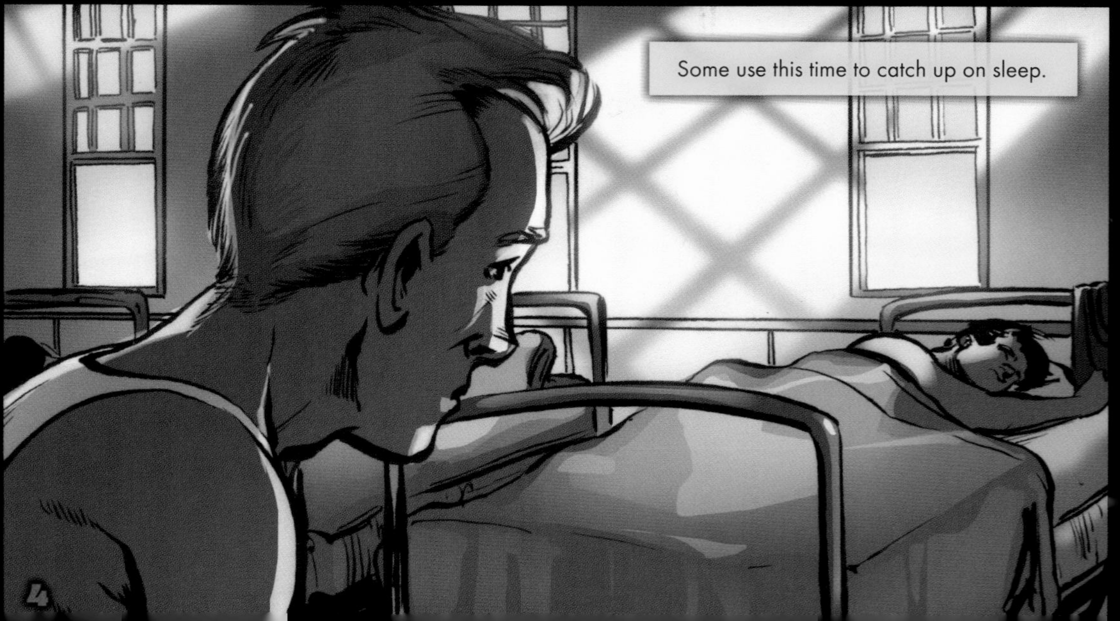
Some use this time to catch up on sleep.

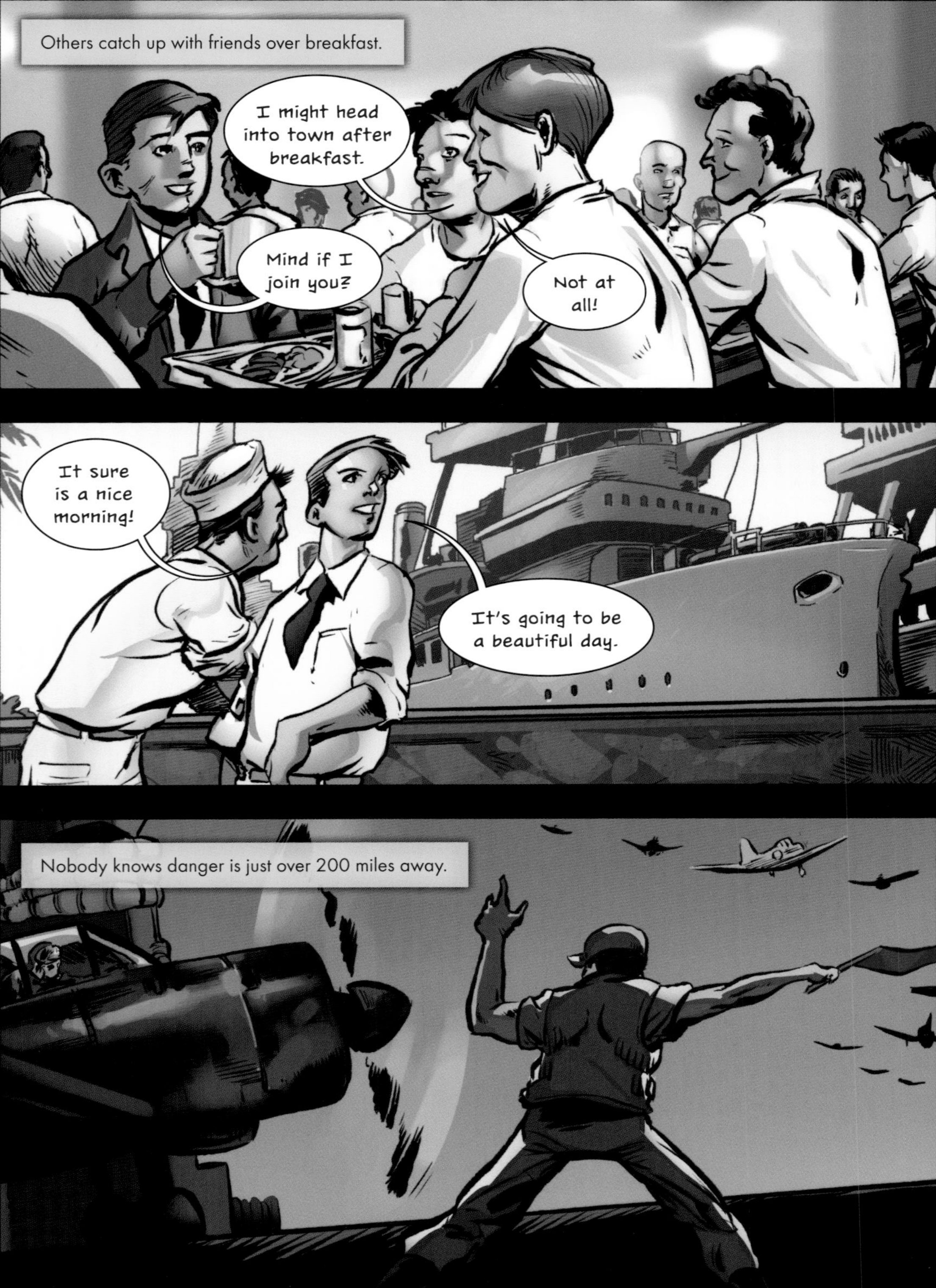
Others catch up with friends over breakfast.
I might head into town after breakfast.
Mind if I join you?
Not at all!
It sure is a nice morning!
It's going to be a beautiful day.
Nobody knows danger is just over 200 miles away.

Tensions Rising

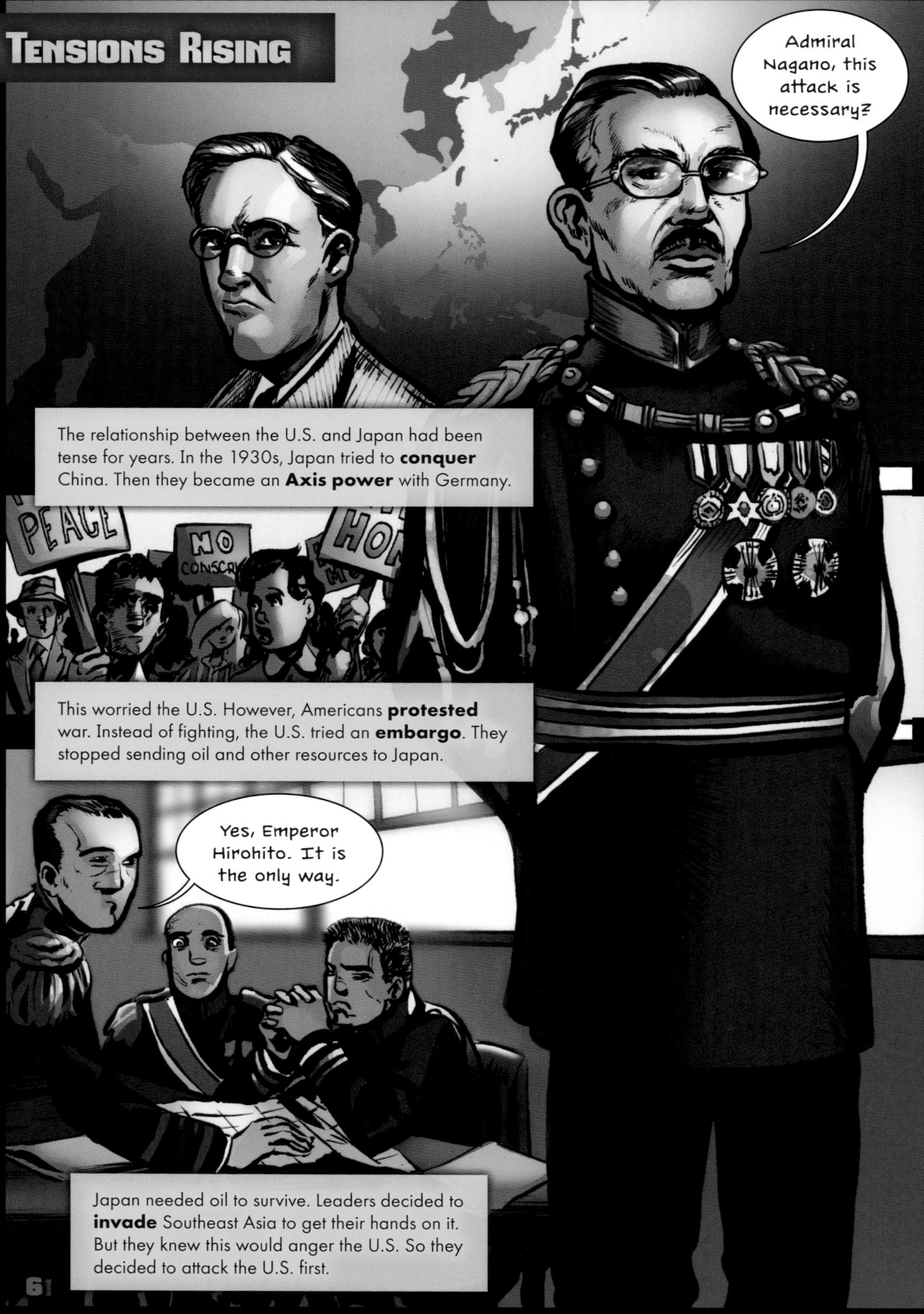
The relationship between the U.S. and Japan had been tense for years. In the 1930s, Japan tried to **conquer** China. Then they became an **Axis power** with Germany.
PEACE
NO CONSCR
This worried the U.S. However, Americans **protested** war. Instead of fighting, the U.S. tried an **embargo**. They stopped sending oil and other resources to Japan.
Admiral Nagano, this attack is necessary?
Yes, Emperor Hirohito. It is the only way.
Japan needed oil to survive. Leaders decided to **invade** Southeast Asia to get their hands on it. But they knew this would anger the U.S. So they decided to attack the U.S. first.

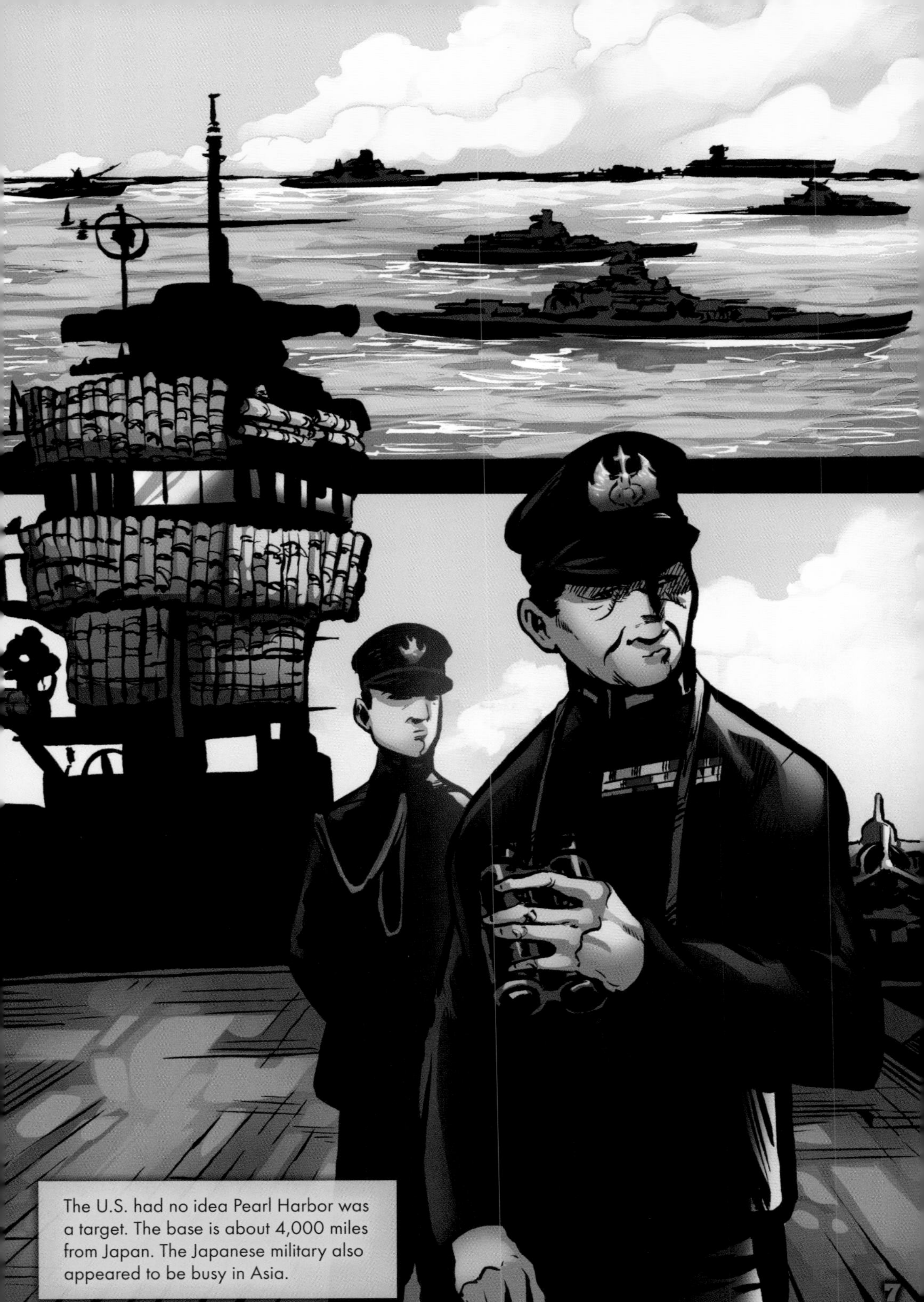
The U.S. had no idea Pearl Harbor was a target. The base is about 4,000 miles from Japan. The Japanese military also appeared to be busy in Asia.

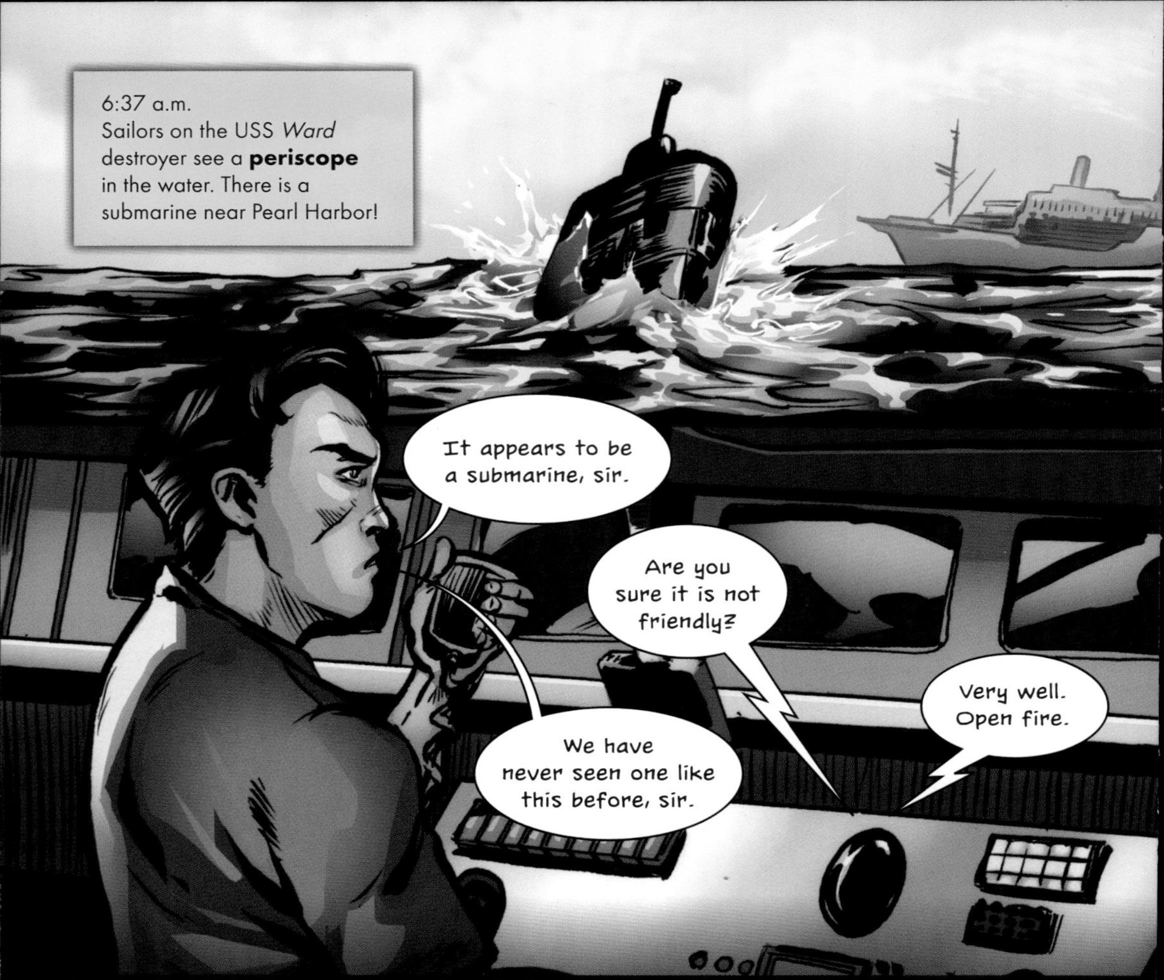
6:37 a.m.
Sailors on the USS *Ward* destroyer see a **periscope** in the water. There is a submarine near Pearl Harbor!
It appears to be a submarine, sir.
Are you sure it is not friendly?
We have never seen one like this before, sir.
Very well. Open fire.

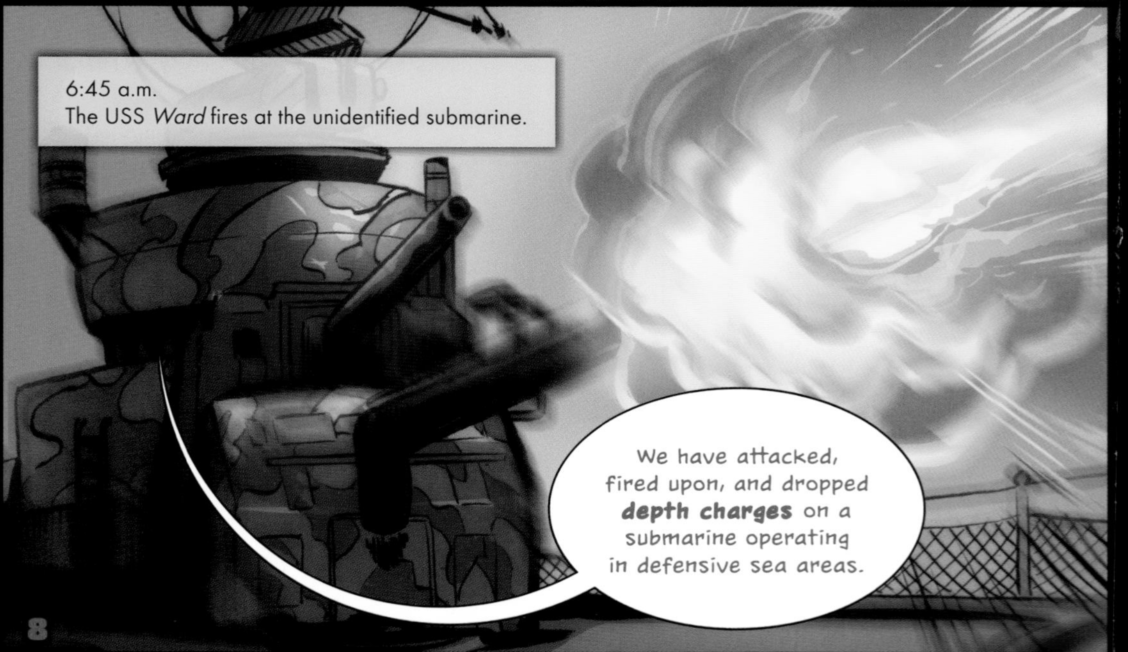
6:45 a.m.
The USS *Ward* fires at the unidentified submarine.
We have attacked, fired upon, and dropped **depth charges** on a submarine operating in defensive sea areas.

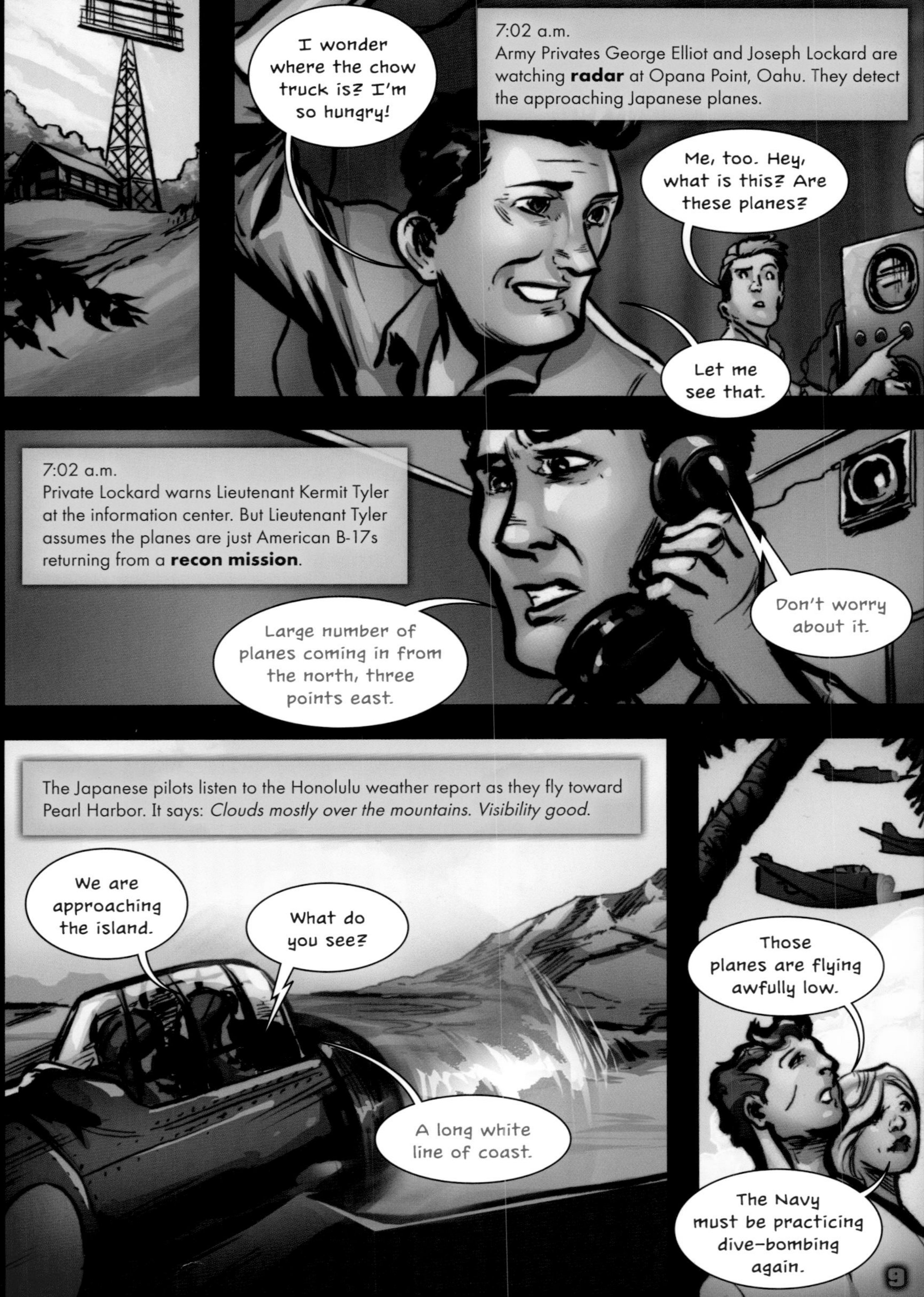
7:02 a.m.
Army Privates George Elliot and Joseph Lockard are watching **radar** at Opana Point, Oahu. They detect the approaching Japanese planes.
I wonder where the chow truck is? I'm so hungry!
Me, too. Hey, what is this? Are these planes?
Let me see that.
7:02 a.m.
Private Lockard warns Lieutenant Kermit Tyler at the information center. But Lieutenant Tyler assumes the planes are just American B-17s returning from a **recon mission**.
Large number of planes coming in from the north, three points east.
Don't worry about it.
The Japanese pilots listen to the Honolulu weather report as they fly toward Pearl Harbor. It says: *Clouds mostly over the mountains. Visibility good.*
We are approaching the island.
What do you see?
A long white line of coast.
Those planes are flying awfully low.
The Navy must be practicing dive-bombing again.

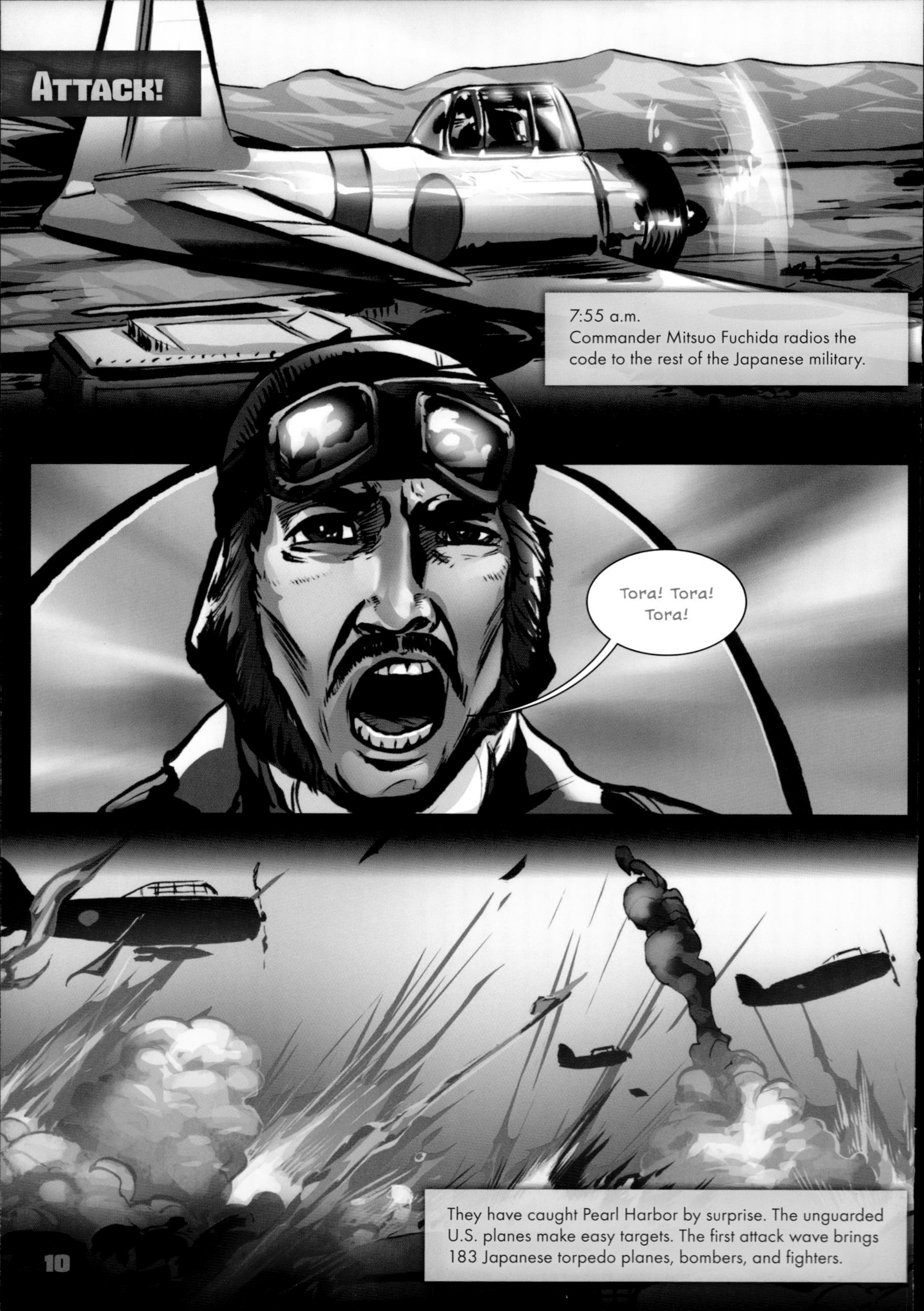
ATTACK!
7:55 a.m.
Commander Mitsuo Fuchida radios the code to the rest of the Japanese military.
Tora! Tora! Tora!
They have caught Pearl Harbor by surprise. The unguarded U.S. planes make easy targets. The first attack wave brings 183 Japanese torpedo planes, bombers, and fighters.

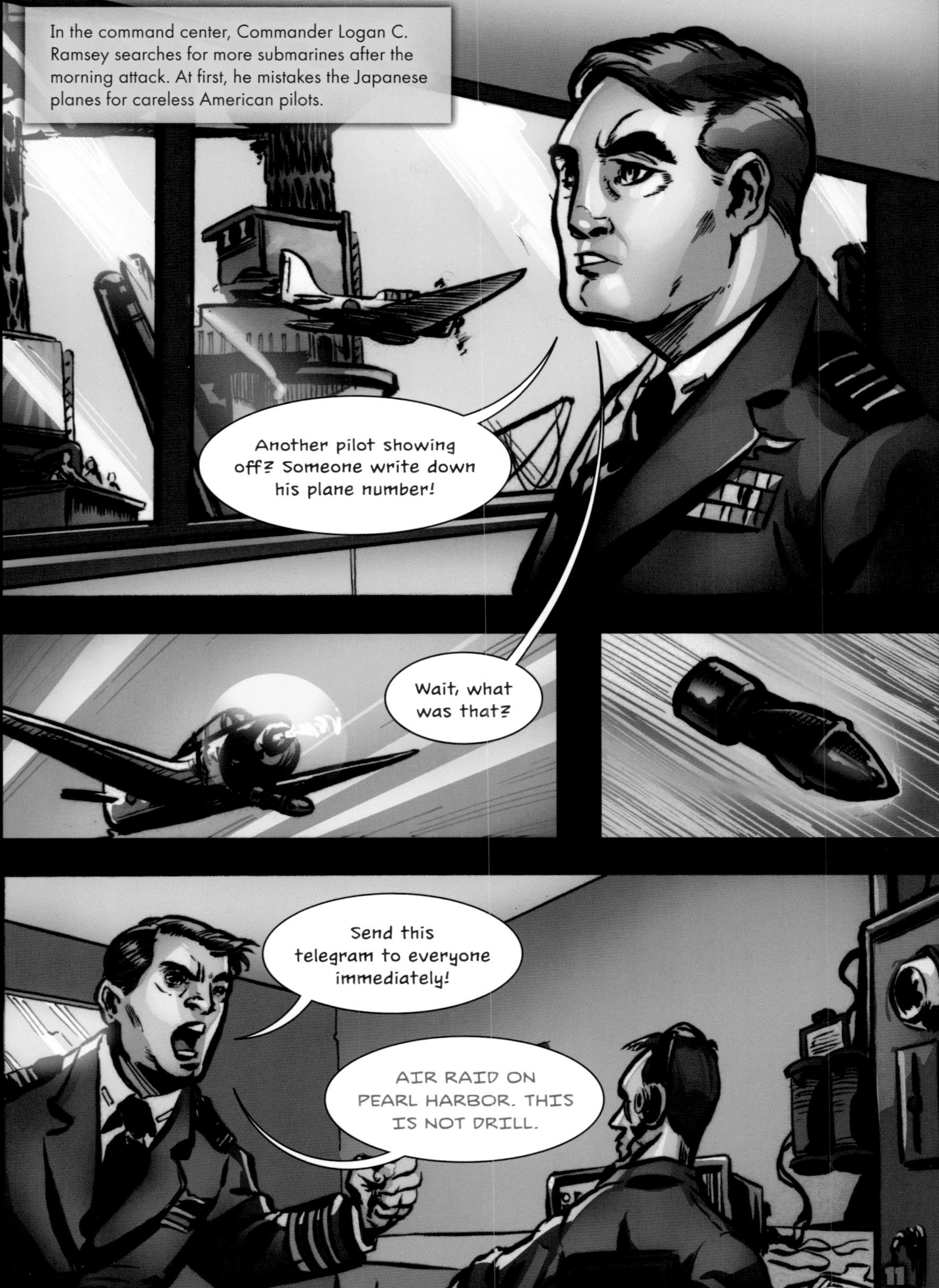
In the command center, Commander Logan C. Ramsey searches for more submarines after the morning attack. At first, he mistakes the Japanese planes for careless American pilots.
Another pilot showing off? Someone write down his plane number!
Wait, what was that?
Send this telegram to everyone immediately!
AIR RAID ON PEARL HARBOR. THIS IS NOT DRILL.

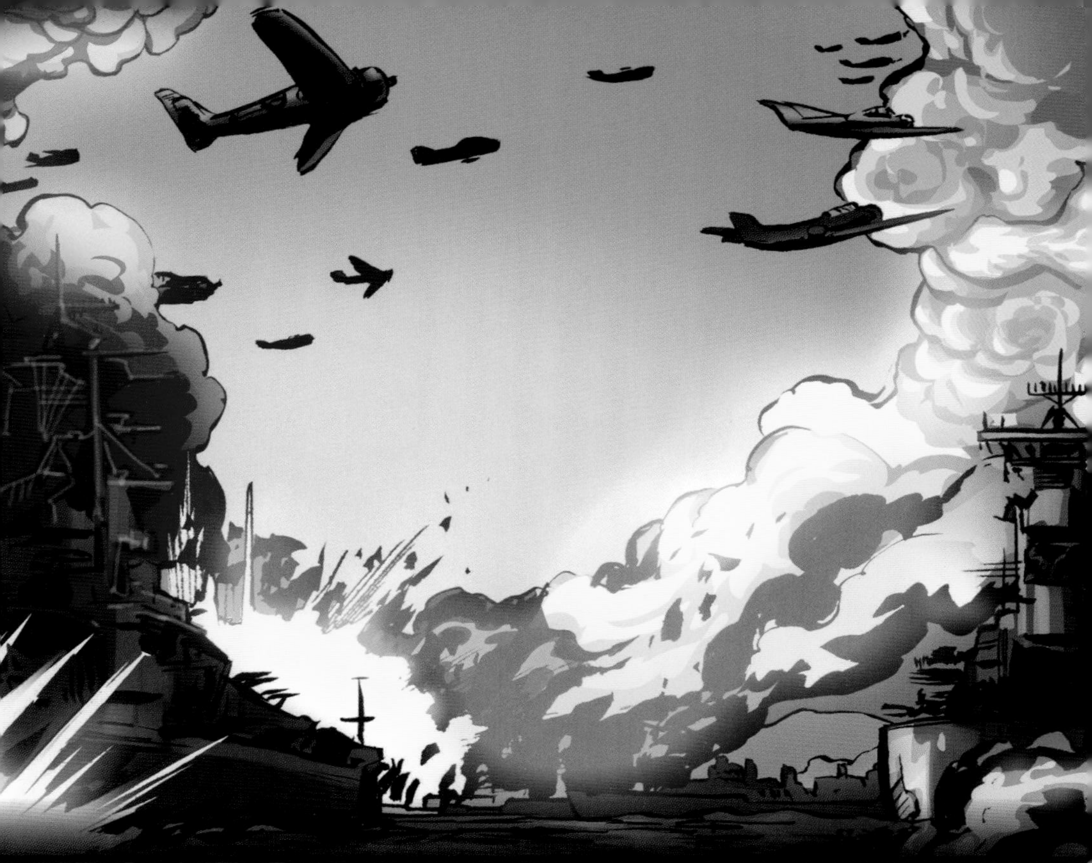

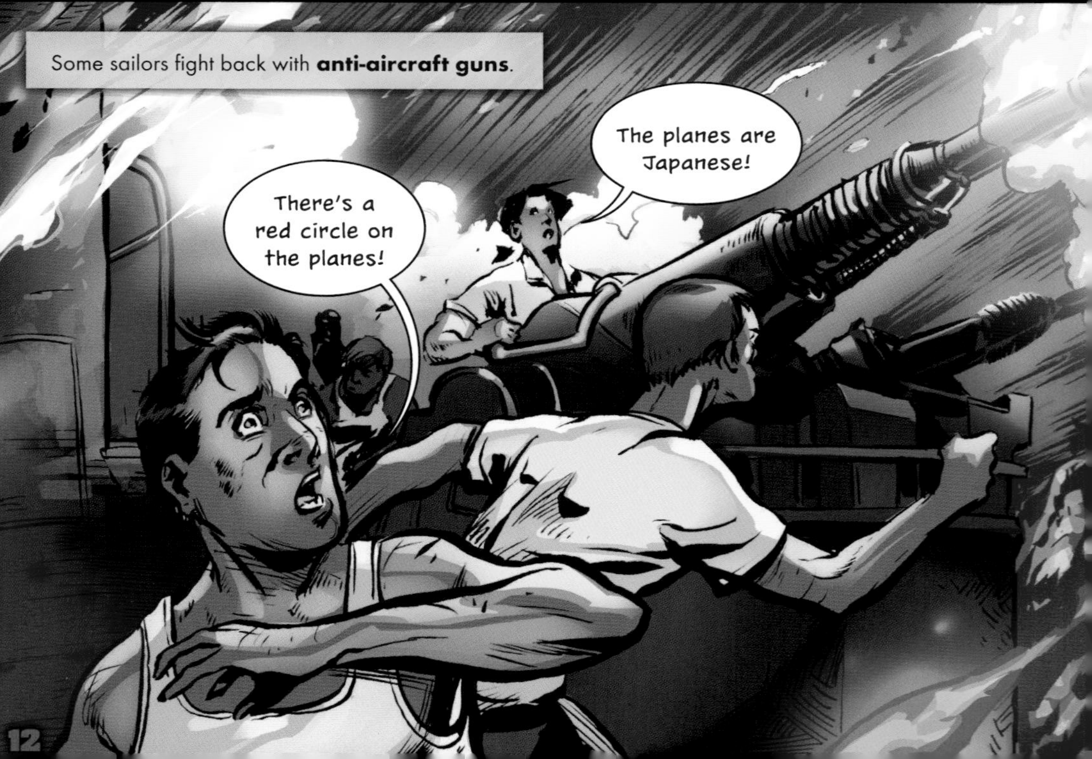
Some sailors fight back with **anti-aircraft guns**.
There's a red circle on the planes!
The planes are Japanese!

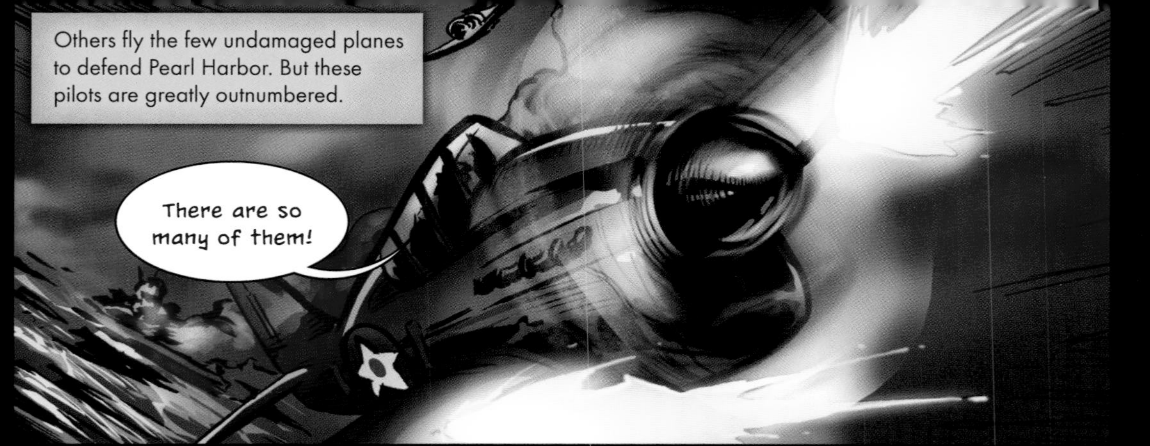
Others fly the few undamaged planes to defend Pearl Harbor. But these pilots are greatly outnumbered.
There are so many of them!

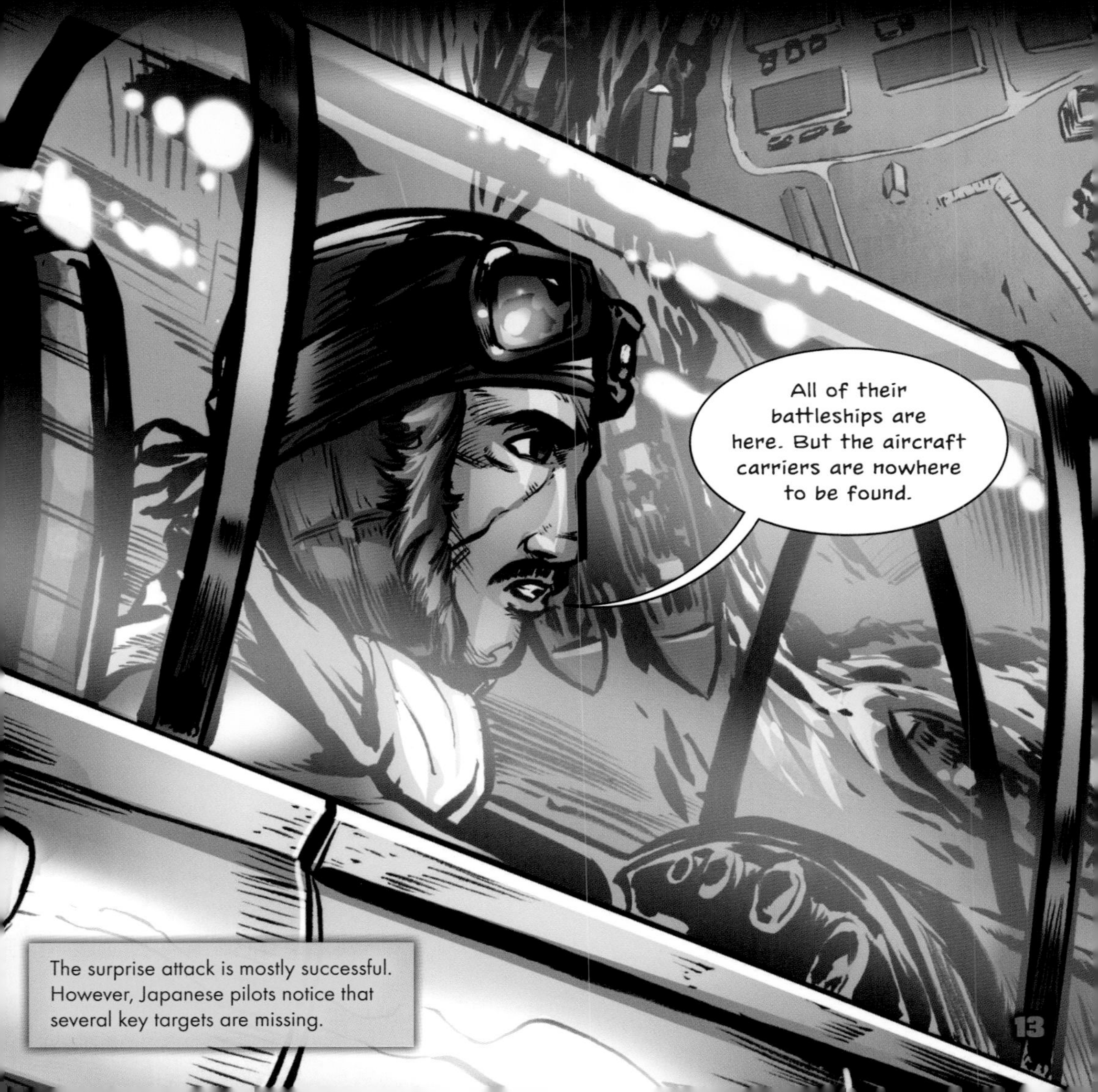
All of their battleships are here. But the aircraft carriers are nowhere to be found.
The surprise attack is mostly successful. However, Japanese pilots notice that several key targets are missing.

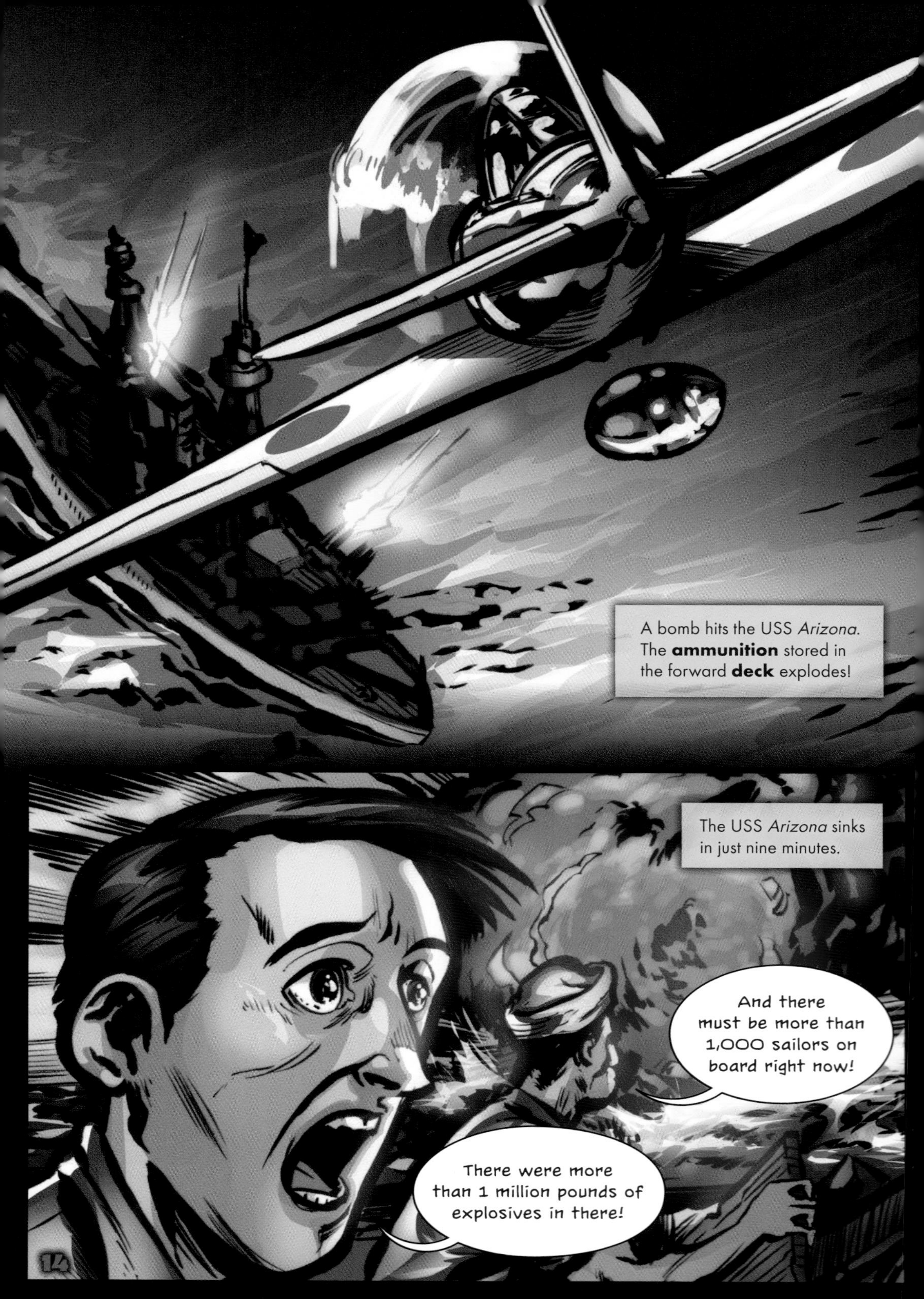
A bomb hits the USS *Arizona*. The **ammunition** stored in the forward **deck** explodes!
The USS *Arizona* sinks in just nine minutes.
There were more than 1 million pounds of explosives in there!
And there must be more than 1,000 sailors on board right now!

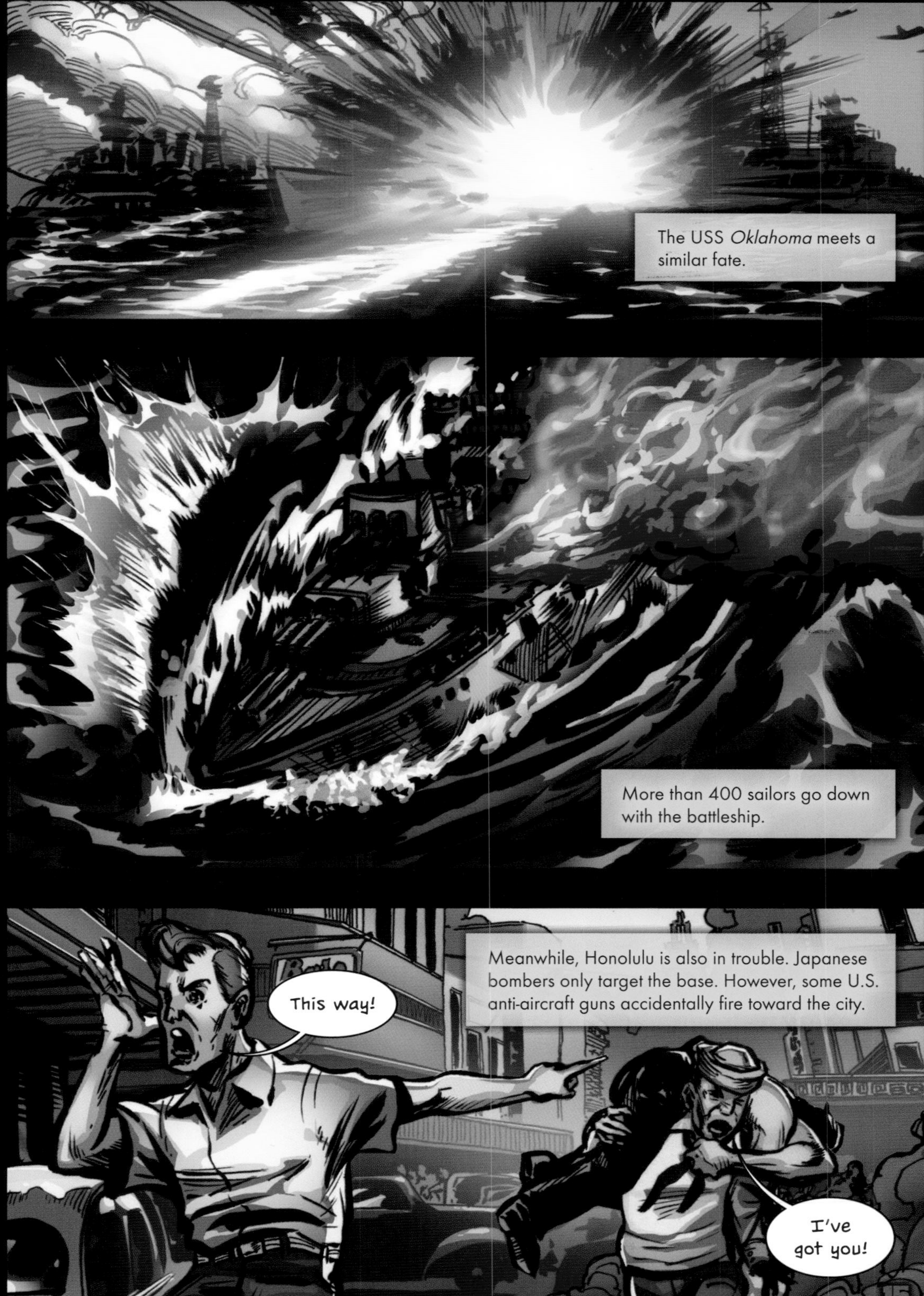
The USS *Oklahoma* meets a similar fate.
More than 400 sailors go down with the battleship.
Meanwhile, Honolulu is also in trouble. Japanese bombers only target the base. However, some U.S. anti-aircraft guns accidentally fire toward the city.
This way!
I've got you!

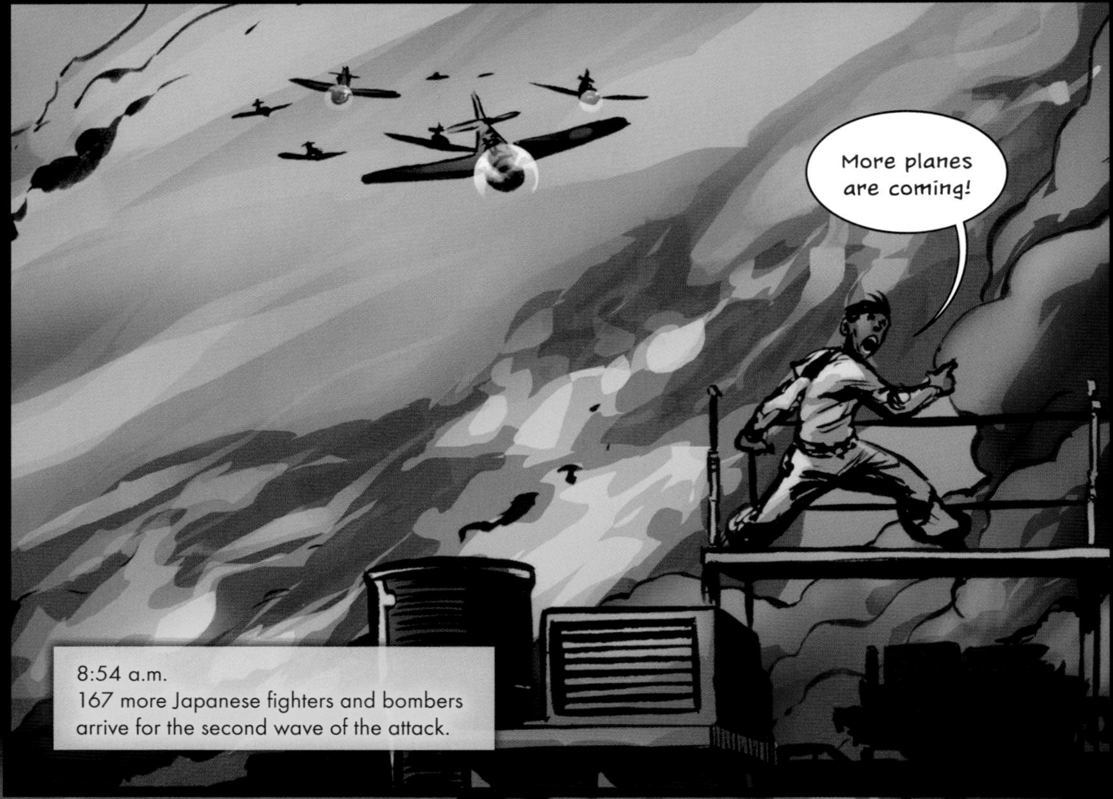
More planes are coming!
8:54 a.m.
167 more Japanese fighters and bombers arrive for the second wave of the attack.

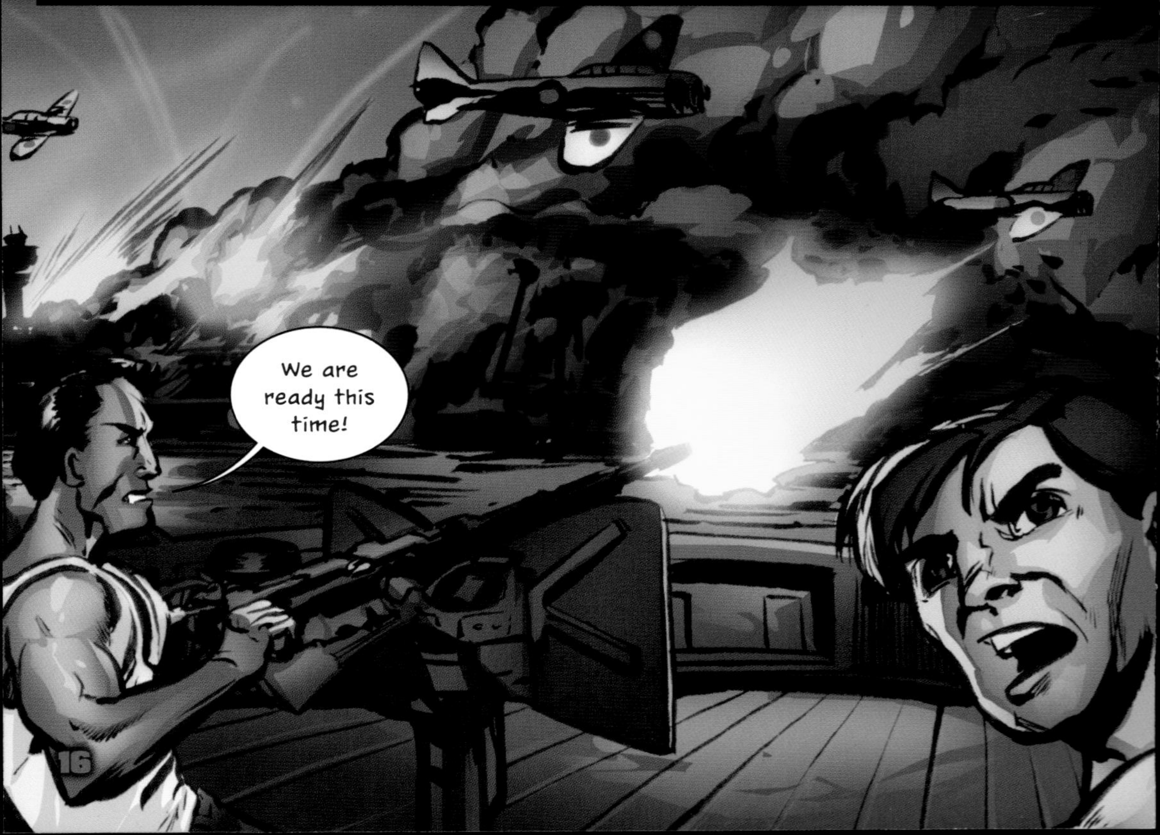
We are ready this time!

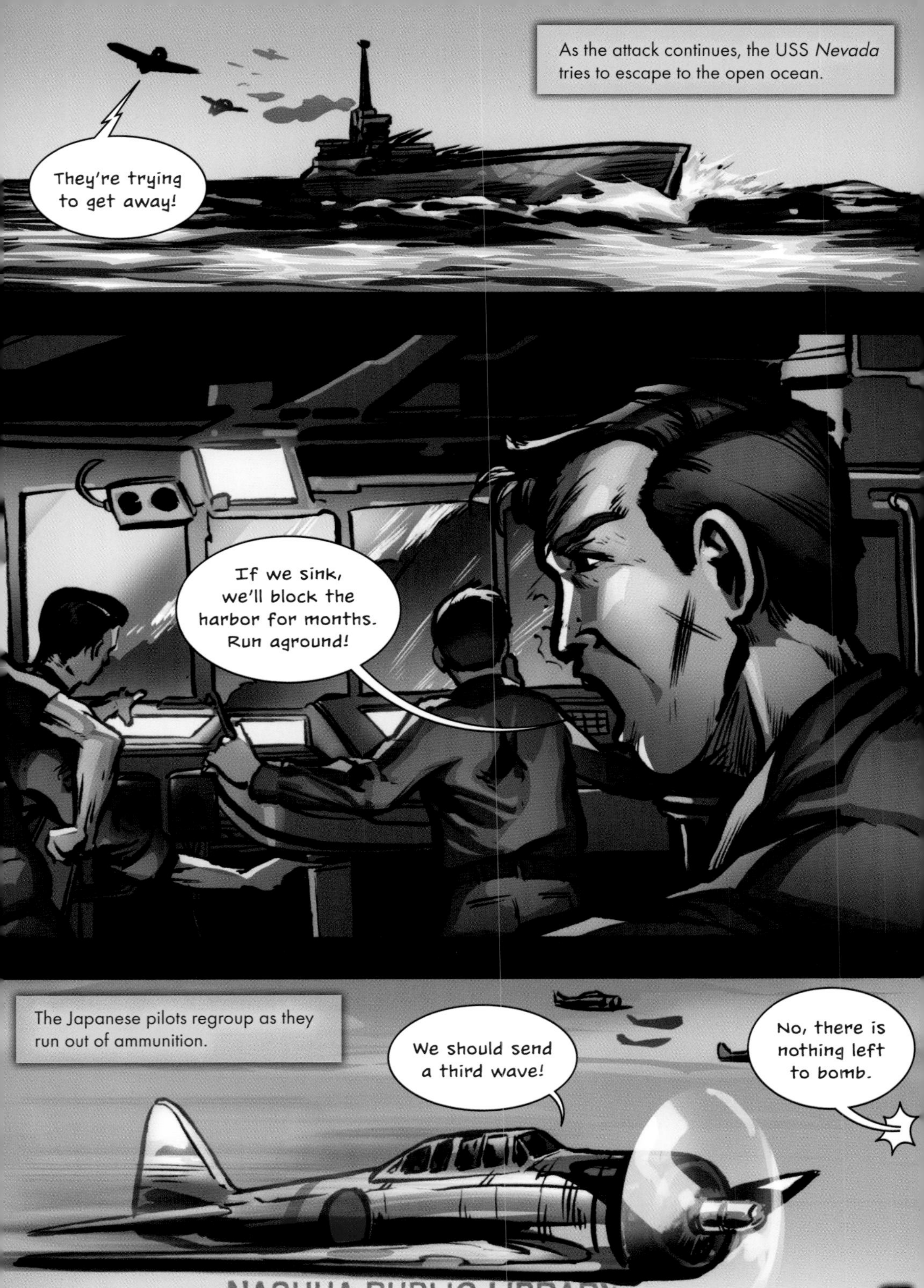
As the attack continues, the USS *Nevada* tries to escape to the open ocean.
They're trying to get away!
If we sink, we'll block the harbor for months. Run aground!
The Japanese pilots regroup as they run out of ammunition.
We should send a third wave!
No, there is nothing left to bomb.

The Aftermath

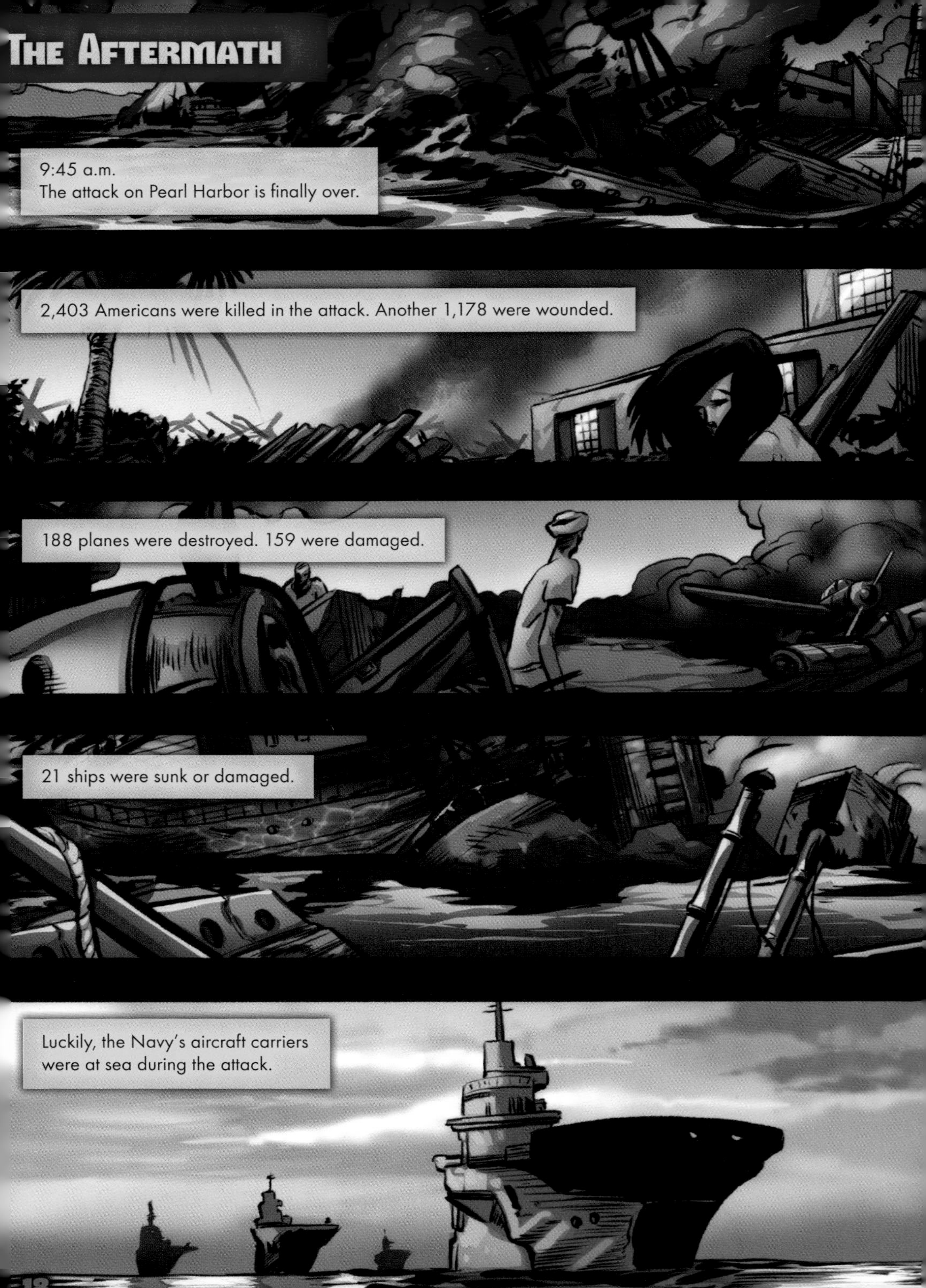
9:45 a.m.
The attack on Pearl Harbor is finally over.
2,403 Americans were killed in the attack. Another 1,178 were wounded.
188 planes were destroyed. 159 were damaged.
21 ships were sunk or damaged.
Luckily, the Navy's aircraft carriers were at sea during the attack.

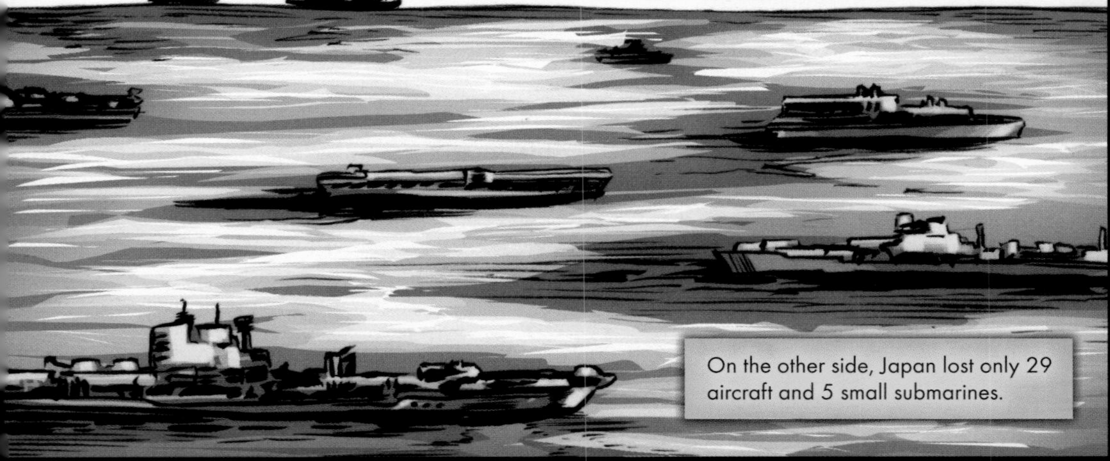
On the other side, Japan lost only 29 aircraft and 5 small submarines.

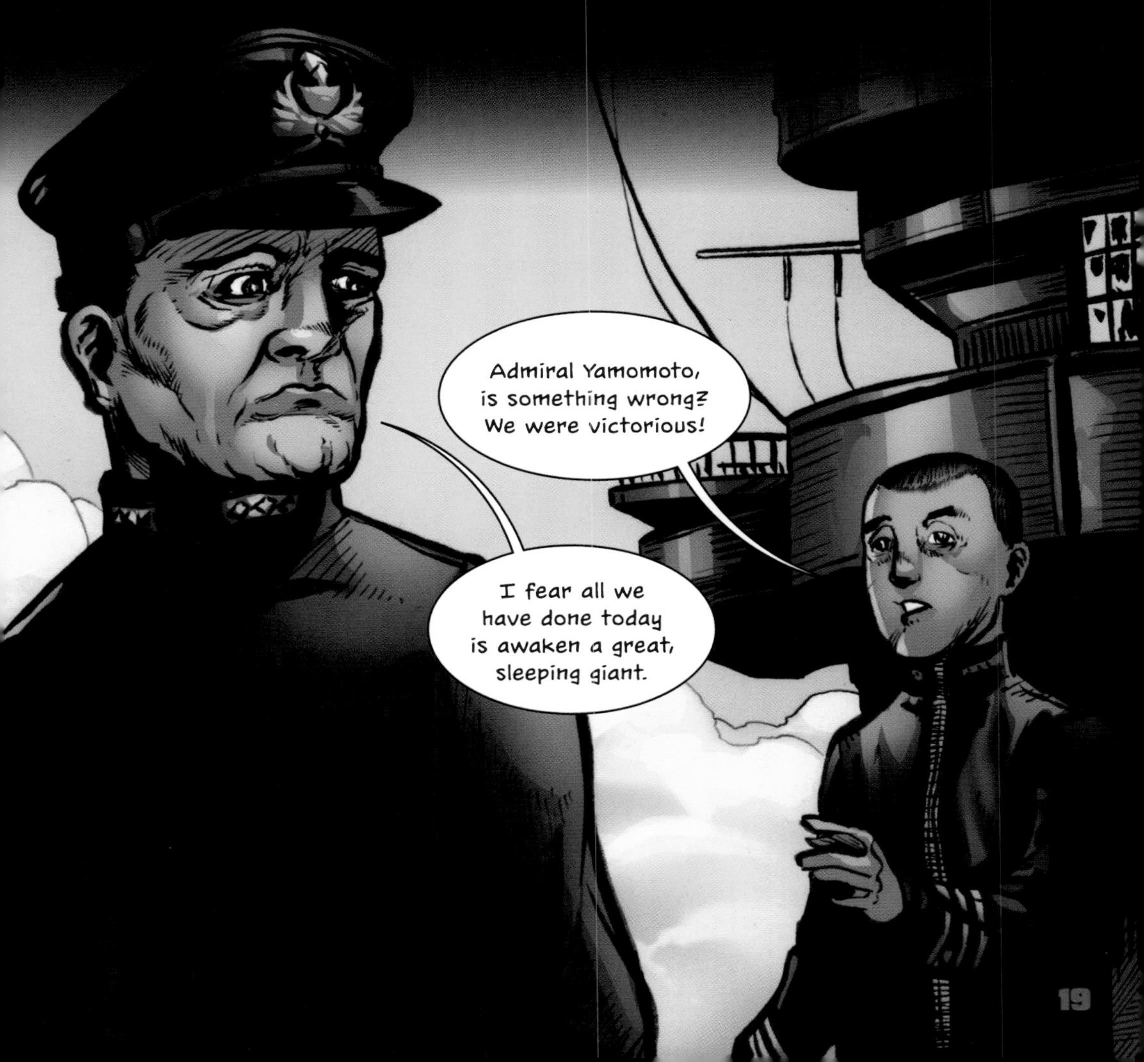
Admiral Yamomoto, is something wrong? We were victorious!
I fear all we have done today is awaken a great, sleeping giant.

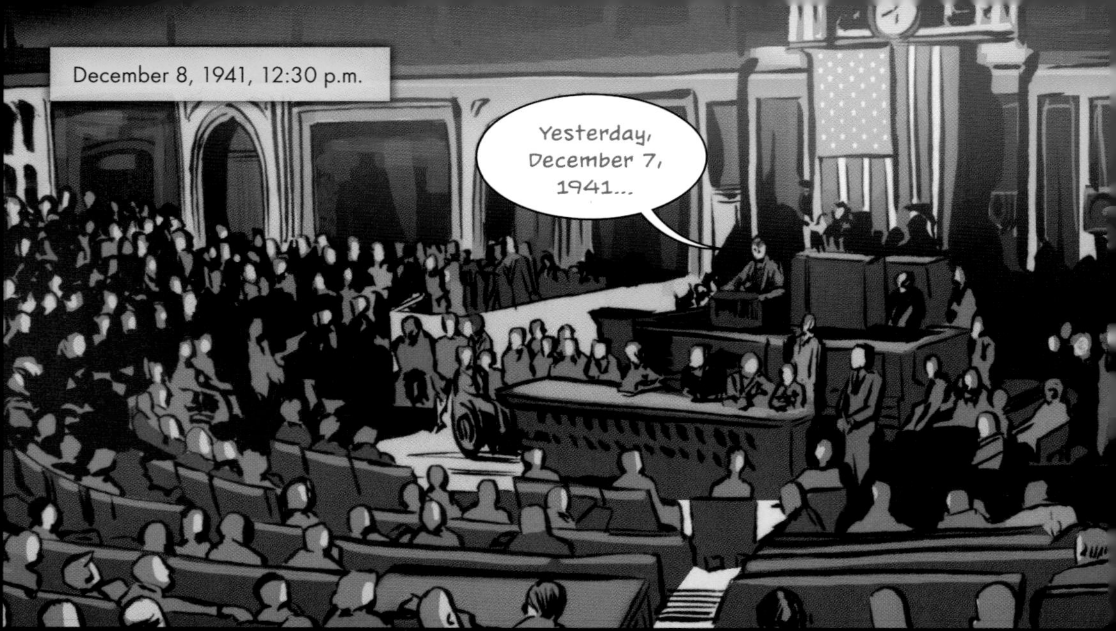
December 8, 1941, 12:30 p.m.
Yesterday, December 7, 1941...

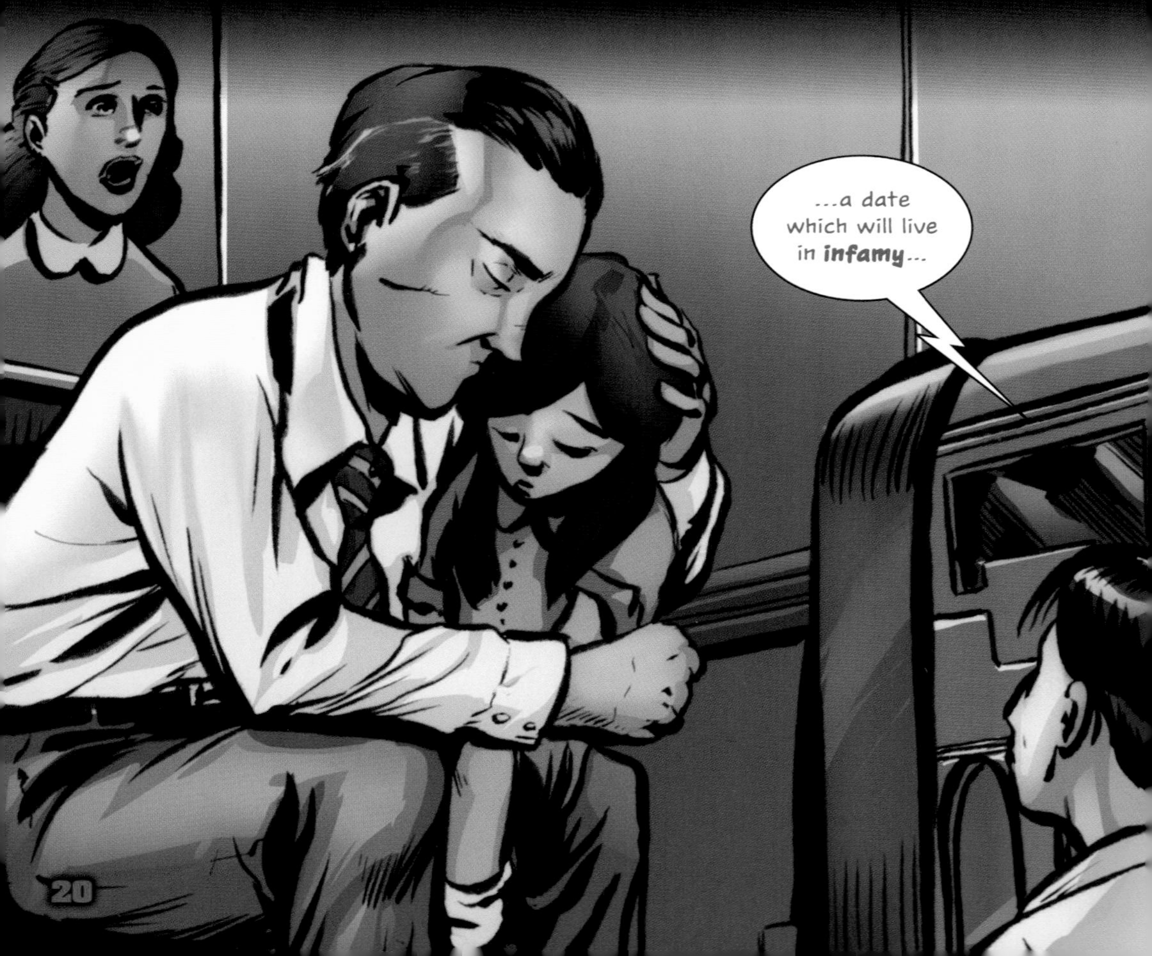
...a date which will live in **infamy**...

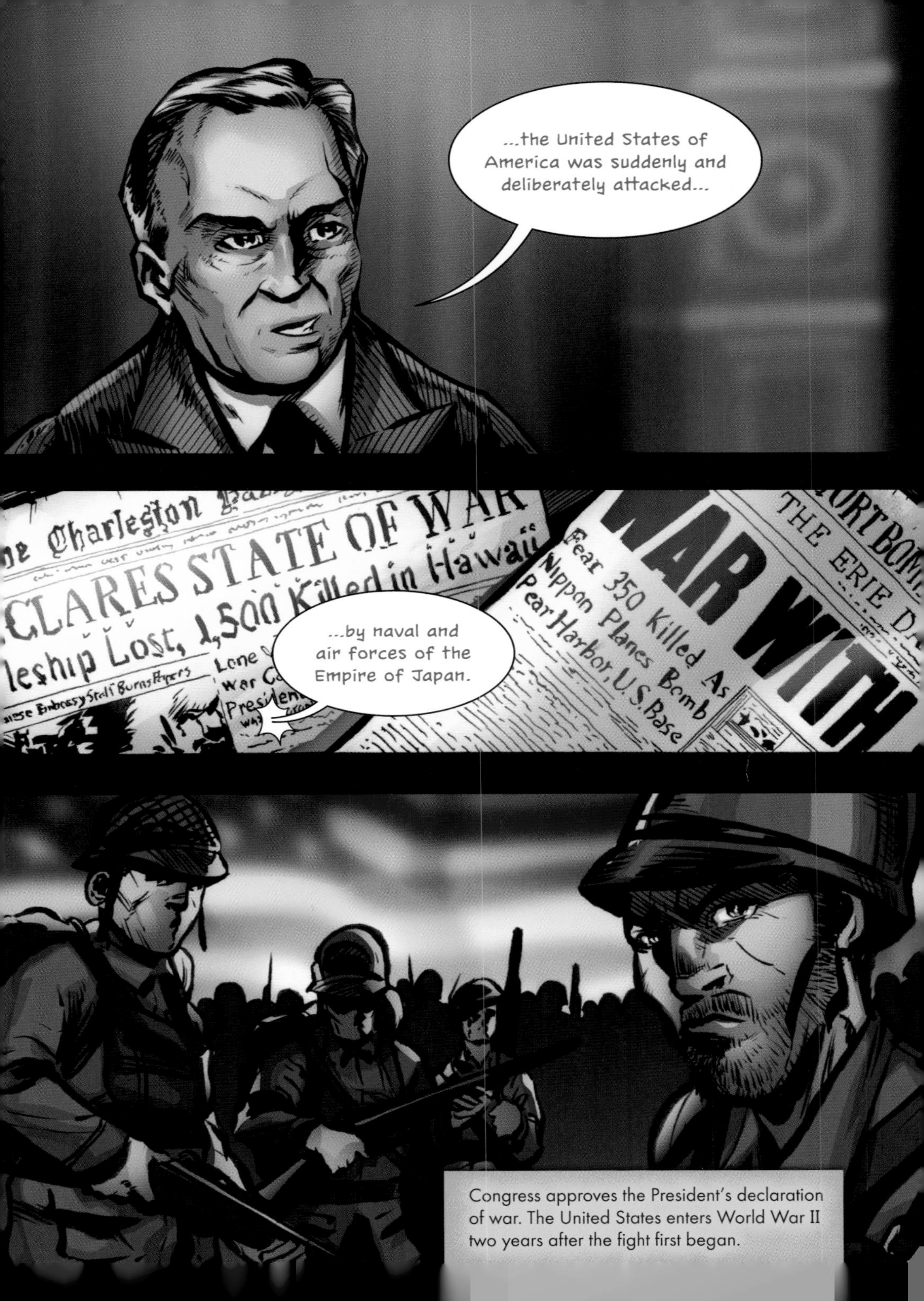
...the United States of America was suddenly and deliberately attacked...
Charleston
CLARES STATE OF WAR
leship Lost, 1,500 Killed in Hawaii
Fear 350 Killed As Nippon Planes Bomb Pear Harbor, U.S. Base
THE ERIE
WAR WITH
...by naval and air forces of the Empire of Japan.
Congress approves the President's declaration of war. The United States enters World War II two years after the fight first began.

MORE ABOUT THE DISASTER

- To avoid being seen, the Japanese ships crossed the northern Pacific Ocean instead of major shipping routes.

- The "long white line of coast" seen by Japanese pilots refers to Oahu's Kakuku Point.

- *Tora! Tora! Tora!* means "Tiger! Tiger! Tiger!" in Japanese. It was the code word that meant they had surprised the U.S.

- The radar station that detected the Japanese planes was fairly new. It had been in operation for less than one month before the attacks.

- One of the U.S. Navy's aircraft carriers, USS *Enterprise*, was supposed to be in Pearl Harbor on the morning of the attack. However, rough seas delayed its arrival until after the attacks.

GLOSSARY

ammunition—bullets or shells that can be shot

anti-aircraft guns—weapons fired at aircraft from the ground or sea

Axis power—a country that fought against the United States in World War II; the Axis powers were Germany, Japan, and Italy.

conquer—to take over by force

deck—a level of a ship or other vessel

depth charges—bombs dropped by ships that explode underwater at a certain depth; depth charges are used to attack submarines.

embargo—a ban on trade with another country

infamy—being well-known for a bad quality or act

invade—to enter a country by force to take control

periscope—an instrument on a submarine used to see above water

protested—publicly disagreed with something

radar—a system used to detect and track planes, ships, and other objects

recon mission—a secret mission used to gather information about an enemy

stationed—assigned to a specific place

To Learn More

AT THE LIBRARY

Lassieur, Allison. *The Attack on Pearl Harbor: An Interactive History Adventure*. Mankato, Minn.: Capstone Press, 2009.

Lemke, Donald. *Captured Off Guard: The Attack on Pearl Harbor*. Minneapolis, Minn.: Stone Arch Books, 2008.

White, Steve. *Day of Infamy: Attack on Pearl Harbor*. New York, N.Y.: Osprey, 2007.

ON THE WEB

Learning more about the attack on Pearl Harbor is as easy as 1, 2, 3.

1. Go to www.factsurfer.com.
2. Enter "attack on Pearl Harbor" into the search box.
3. Click the "Surf" button and you will see a list of related web sites.

With factsurfer.com, finding more information is just a click away.

INDEX